THE
BIBLE
STORY

One Story
from **GENESIS** *to* **REVELATION**

PREBEN VANG

ACADEMIC
NASHVILLE, TENNESSEE

The Bible Story
Copyright © 2019 by Preben Vang

Published by B&H Academic
Nashville, Tennessee

ISBN: 978-1-5359-9502-3

Dewey Decimal Classification: 220.95
Subject Heading: BIBLE STORIES / BIBLE—STUDY
AND TEACHING / BIBLE—CHRONOLOGY

Printed in the United States of America

1 2 3 4 5 6 7 8 9 10 • 24 23 22 21 20 19

VP

The Bible Story
One Story from Genesis to Revelation

Creation and Identity

The story of the Bible begins with God. In the beginning, God created the universe. God is not a part of the universe as a mere power; he is a separate and independent Creator who deliberately created everything that exists. Being an expression of God's own beauty, love, and relational character, creation belongs to God. Everything in creation, therefore, from the smallest and seemingly most insignificant to God's crowning work, the human being, finds its meaning, identity, and reason for existence in the relationship between the Creator and his creation.

Image and Presence

To express his love, God decided to give to creation an expression of his own image—the human being. He created the human being as man and woman and gave them managerial power over the rest of creation. They were to live in a close and loving relationship with their Creator and conduct their lives as an expression of that relationship. Human beings, however, decided they could live on their own, without God. This decision destroyed the intimacy of their relationship with the Creator, and as their relationship deteriorated, the image of God faded, and humans lost the true quality of their humanity.

Alienation and Separation

Outside God's presence, human beings experienced the results of the destroyed fellowship with God. Blessing had been exchanged for curse. Envy, pain, and evil (even to the point of murder) became commonplace. Humans proved that the goodness and love that came from the presence of God were annihilated by their own desire to put themselves first. Sin, which in its essence is the rebellion of humans against

God, had become the governing quality of humankind. Evil grew and covered the earth; God was forgotten.

Grace and Promise

The never-ending grace of God, however, would not let go of his crowning work of the creation. Rather than withdrawing, God established a new covenantal relationship with humankind. A man named Abraham, who is now considered the father of faith (Luke 16:24; Rom 4:16–5:2; Heb 11:17) because of his unwavering trust in God, received a promise that his numerous descendants would be blessed. In fact, blessing would come to the whole earth through them. Because of this covenant promise given to Abraham, all the people of the earth would have the opportunity to experience the blessing of God's presence once again.

Unilateral Covenant with Abraham

The promise to Abraham was a unilateral promise; that is, it was a promise from God with no condition placed on humans. It was an expression of pure grace; God placed it solely upon himself to reestablish the relationship with the rebellious creatures he originally had created in his own image. In this way, the Abrahamic covenant became the basis for the salvation of human beings. Again and again, in spite of the repeated attempts by humans to destroy their relationship with the Creator, God remembered his covenant with Abraham and opened a door for humans to find their way back into his presence.

Promise and People

At first it looked as if God's promise was empty; Abraham was without children. But in Abraham's old age, God granted him a son of promise, Isaac, who in turn became the father of Jacob. Jacob, whom God later renamed Israel, had twelve sons, whose names would later give rise to the names of Israel's twelve tribes. God had created for himself a people called Israel. This people, also called the Hebrews, were to be recognized and characterized by their trust in the one God, the creator of heaven and earth.

Identity and Presence

Famine came upon the land, and the family of Jacob went to Egypt to find food. In Egypt, the people of Israel increased in number; and as time passed, the Egyptian rulers, called pharaohs, worried that the Israelites would become too powerful. To counter this threat, the pharaohs enslaved the descendants of Jacob. For approximately 400 years, the faithful among the people cried to God for help in their misery. In these darkest of days, an Egyptian princess fell in love with one of the Israelite babies named Moses. She took him as her son and raised him as an Egyptian prince. When he came of age, Moses realized his Hebrew heritage, and he left Egypt to live in the desert.

God's Self-Revelation

Remembering his covenant with Abraham, God called Moses in the desert and charged him with the task of liberating his people from their bondage in Egypt. Moses refused, arguing that he did not even know the name of Israel's God. At a burning bush, God revealed himself to

Moses as Yahweh, the *I AM*, the One who is always present with his people.

Power and Judgment

Moses returned to Egypt imploring Pharaoh to let the Hebrews go, but Pharaoh would not listen. Plagues sent by God invaded the land, but Pharaoh still did not listen. Even when God gave his last warning, Pharaoh's heart and mind remained unmoved. God warned that he would send an angel of death to visit every household in Egypt and kill the firstborn of all families unless Pharaoh released Israel from slavery and allowed them to leave Egypt to worship God in the desert.

Passover and Salvation

To avoid death among the families of Israel, God told his people to make a meal in haste. Each family were to take the blood of a lamb and smear it on their door frame to let the angel of death know that he was to *pass over* their home. God would save his people by the blood of the lamb.

Salvation and Freedom

After this final plague, Egypt let Israel go. They even hurried them along. Israel left and came to the Sea of Reeds. By this time, the Egyptians regretted their decision to release their slaves, and they sent out armies to take them back. The Hebrews found themselves caught between the water and the Egyptian army. They were trapped; the only way of escape went through the water—an impossible situation.

Exodus and Guidance

God kept his promise to Abraham, however, and opened the waters for his people to cross to the other side of the sea. The Egyptians, close behind, drowned on the bottom of the sea when God closed the waters as soon as Israel had passed through. God had rescued his people! He had created for them an exodus—a way out of slavery. They were now on their way to the land God had promised them. They were free to follow him and to live in his presence. He would guide them through the desert by a cloud during the day and a pillar of fire during the night.

A new situation had become a reality for Israel. Yahweh was in the midst of his people; the holy Creator God lived among humans. He dwelled among them in a tabernacle— a portable tent designed for worship, the celebration of God's presence.

Bilateral Covenant with Moses

How were people to live in this new situation? What guidelines should govern this new relationship? God called Moses to a mountaintop and gave him a set of ten guiding rules for Israel. These regulations, called the Ten Commandments, became the foundation for a new bilateral covenant called the Mosaic covenant. It was bilateral because demands were put on both parties in the relationship. Yahweh promised he would be their God, they would be his people, and he would dwell in their midst. They were to keep the law as expressed in the commandments. Beyond the Ten Commandments, other rules and regulations were written down to define how the Israelites should live and worship the God in their midst. As a legal covenant, the Mosaic covenant required man's obedience as its central feature. This was different from the Abrahamic covenant, which had God's faithfulness to his promise as its central feature.

Rebellion and Judgment

As usual, God kept his end of the agreement. He led the people to the edge of the land promised to Abraham—Canaan; but when they arrived, they were afraid to take possession of the land. This lack of trust in God sent them back into the desert to wander for forty years. Only after that faithless generation had died off did Yahweh again lead them to enter the land. After Moses's death, Joshua became the leader of the people. He led them to victory after victory until they took possession of the land God had promised them.

Judges and Misery

Following Joshua's death in the Promised Land, a series of judges became leaders of the Israelites. Men and women such as Gideon, Deborah, and Samson led Israel's armies and passed judgment on the people. This is sometimes considered the dark age of Hebrew history. Not only did many of the Israelites stop worshipping Yahweh, but several of the judges were active in worshipping idols. It was a dark day for the relationship between God and his people. But, as before, God put an end to the misery of Israel. The time of the judges drew to an end as Israel demanded a human king. They wanted to be like the other nations.

Kings and God

During the reign of their second king, King David, the Abrahamic covenant—with its promise of land, blessing, and peace for Israel—came close to a complete fulfillment. David was Yahweh's answer to the destitution caused by the period of the judges. He was a man after God's own heart, a shepherd boy whose greatest desire was to please God. Under David, the kingdom grew to a hitherto unknown size and greatness. David made Jerusalem the capital of Israel and sought to build Yahweh a temple. This task, however, fell to his son, Solomon.

The Unilateral Davidic Covenant

Nonetheless, God was pleased with David's desire to build a temple for Yahweh's presence among his people, so he extended a covenant promise to David. God promised to make David's name great, grant an eternal place for his people, and establish a permanent dynasty in the Davidic line. This Davidic covenant, like the Abrahamic, was a unilateral covenant with no condition placed on humans for its fulfillment. It forms the basis for Israel's hope, as later expressed by the prophets and most climactically underscored in the genealogies of Jesus.

God's Temple, Solomon, and the Division of God's People

Solomon, who followed his father David as king, became world-renowned for his wisdom and incredible wealth. Out of this wealth, he built Yahweh a temple in Jerusalem. Upon its completion, the Bible explains how God filled the temple with his presence. However, Solomon disobeyed God and did not have the heart of his father. Solomon's sin led to the split of the kingdom after his death. Ten tribes followed Jeroboam, a former general under Solomon, who established the kingdom of Israel in the north; two tribes stayed with Rehoboam, Solomon's son, to establish the kingdom of Judah in the south. These two nations picked up where the judges left off and continued the destruction of their relationship with God. Even priests replaced the worship of Yahweh with the worship of Baal, a Canaanite god. The people seemed intent on breaking the Mosaic covenant.

The Prophets and Their Message

During this time, the eighth century before Christ, prophets spoke out from both the north and the south, warning the people of the imminent judgment of God. The prophetic message proclaimed God's indictment on the people. God's people had violated the covenant by their idolatry, their social injustice, and their religious formalism. "You have broken the covenant," the prophets charged. "You must repent! If there is no repentance, judgment will come!" And judgment came! The Assyrians destroyed the northern kingdom of Israel in 721 BC; and Babylon destroyed Judah in 586 BC, forcing a large number of Hebrews into exile in Babylon. The people had broken their covenantal relationship with God. They now had to rely solely on the hope of restoration, which had always been part of the prophetic message.

The Exile and the New Covenant Promise

During the exile, the focus of the people changed. Prophets such as Ezekiel (like Jeremiah before him) looked forward to a time when God's law no longer would be written on tablets of stone but on human hearts—a time when God's Spirit would indwell every member of God's family to ensure an internal drawing toward God's word and will. "God will establish a new covenant with his people," they proclaimed.

Daniel, a devout young man from Judah, who counseled the king of Babylon during the exile, saw a vision of someone like a Son of Man, who possessed authority and who would one day create an everlasting kingdom. People from all nations and all languages would come to worship this Son of Man. It was a time of renewed hope.

God's Presence Beyond the Temple

The Mosaic covenant was shattered, but the prophets were looking back to the unilateral covenants given to Abraham and David. God would no longer limit his presence to the temple in Jerusalem. Ezekiel shared a vision in which God's throne was on wheels, moving in every direction. In the days to come, God would move with his people as in the days of old—not just among them, as with the tabernacle, but within them, through his Spirit. The glory that had left the temple would be manifested through the people of the Spirit.

Exile and Return

When Persia conquered Babylon, the Persians allowed the people of Israel to return to their homeland. After seventy years of exile, Zerubbabel led God's people back to the Promised Land to rebuild the temple. The restoration of the wall around Jerusalem and the reestablishment of the full worship of Yahweh came later, under the leadership of Nehemiah and Ezra. These leaders of Israel made great efforts to bring Israel back to preexilic times. But it never happened. Yahweh did not return to fill the temple with his presence as he had done under Solomon. The nation of Israel did not become truly independent.

A New Covenant is Coming

The Mosaic covenant had been broken, and it would not be restored. The law no longer defined the covenant relationship between God and his people; it functioned simply as a rigorous guideline for living. The period after the exile, the so-called postexilic period, functioned as an interim time between the judgment of the exile and the promise of a new covenant restoration. It was a time in which God, once again, would be visible among his people. This new covenant, which prophets like Jeremiah, Joel, and others had prophesied about, was to be a covenant of the Spirit.

Breaking God's Bilateral Covenant with Moses

The people had broken the bilateral Mosaic covenant, but God remembered his covenant with Abraham and David. In the fullness of time, some 400 years later, he sent his own Son in the form of a human to fulfill the promises of blessing to the world and eternal kingship on David's throne. The New Testament begins its story by placing this Son in the lineage of both David and Abraham.

The Forerunner for the Messiah

An angel of God visited a priest named Zechariah while he was ministering in the temple and told him that his aged wife, Elizabeth, would give birth to a son, who would be great in the eyes of God. The child, John, who became known as John the Baptist (or the Baptizer), served as the forerunner to the Messiah. His purpose was to announce to the people that the new covenant relationship God had promised was at hand. John the Baptist, in other words, served as a prophetic bridge between the old and new covenants.

The Announcement of the Messiah

God's angel, Gabriel, visited a young girl from Judah named Mary and told her that God's own Spirit would overshadow her and make her pregnant. The child to come was to be called Jesus, which means "Savior." He would become the long-awaited Messiah, whom the prophets had spoken about and looked for to save the world.

God's Public Announcement of Jesus as the Messiah

Jesus was born in simple circumstances and grew in wisdom, stature, and favor with God and man. At about thirty years of age, Jesus went to the desert where John the Baptist was preaching and baptizing, and he asked John to baptize him. Coming up from the water, God initiated Jesus's ministry when the Holy Spirit descended upon him in the form of a dove; and God spoke the words, "This is my beloved Son. I take delight in Him!"

Jesus's Message and God's Kingdom

Everywhere he went, Jesus preached the message that God's kingdom had come near. For three years he walked and taught. His message was consistent in both word and deed. God's kingdom had come near. Some people were confused, however, because their expectations of the promised Messiah were so different from what they saw in Jesus. Even John the Baptist, who himself had looked forward to God's intervention, became confused and sent his disciples to ask

Jesus if he was the one to come. Jesus sent these words back to John the Baptist: "Tell John what you have seen and heard. The blind receive sight, the lame walk, those with leprosy are cured, the deaf hear, the dead are raised, and the good news is preached to the poor."

Jesus's Ministry and God's Presence

The evidence was abundantly clear: God had come back to dwell among his people. His power overflowed, and the message of his presence was again proclaimed. The old prophetic indictment and warning that the people were destroying the covenant had been replaced by the proclamation that God was fulfilling his promise. God would establish his presence among his people. Jesus's message sounded just as clear as that of the prophets of old. God wants his people for himself; there is no room for idolatry. "You must repent," Jesus said. God has no pleasure in religious formalism. What matters, said Jesus, is the heart. New covenant worshippers will worship in Spirit and in truth. God still hates social injustice. Jesus came to preach good news to the poor and to release the oppressed.

Jesus's Last Supper and the New Covenant

For the Jewish leaders, Jesus's message served as a radical indictment of their lifestyle, beliefs, and position. They plotted to kill Jesus and put an end to his growing group of disciples. It all came to a head during a week of Passover celebration. Jesus assembled his twelve closest disciples in an upper room to celebrate the Jewish Passover. Knowing what was about to happen, he told them of his imminent death.

Gathered around the Passover table for a meal designed to remember how God had saved his people from slavery in Egypt, Jesus changed the symbolic content of the typical Jewish Passover meal and made it a celebration of the new covenant. Jesus took the bread and broke it, saying that it represented his body, which was about to be broken for many. He also poured the wine, saying that it represented his blood, which was about to be shed for the forgiveness of sin.

Jesus's Death and God's Pain

Later that evening, he went to the garden of Gethsemane to pray. As he was praying, the Jewish leaders, escorted by

Judas and a large number of soldiers, came to take him captive. After an illegal trial before the Jewish Sanhedrin, Jesus stood before the Roman prefect Pontius Pilate for a Roman trial. Though Pilate found Jesus not guilty, he still gave in to the pressure of the Jewish leaders, who had stirred up the crowd against Jesus.

Jesus was crucified on Friday—killed by the cruelest and most painful method of execution known to the Romans. That same day, when Jesus died, the pain of God, giving his own Son for the sins of humankind, became evident. The sun darkened, and the temple's curtain, which separated the temple's holy area from its most holy area, tore from top to bottom. It was as if God had torn his clothes to express his own pain and suffering. At the same time, God had created open access into the place of his holy dwelling.

Jesus's Resurrection and Death's Defeat

Jesus's death on the cross was not God's final word, however. By his sacrificial death, Jesus paid the price for the sins of humankind, opening the door for people again to enjoy the fellowship with God that sin had broken. Jesus died not just as a religious man but as the Son of God. God majestically and powerfully confirmed Jesus as his Son when Jesus rose from the dead on the third day. The resurrection vindicated Jesus's death as an act of God and verified his identity as the Son of God. As Paul would later say, without the resurrection, faith in Jesus would have been meaningless. But as it is, because Jesus did rise, faith in him means everything. It reestablishes a saving relationship between God and humans who put their trust in him.

Jesus's Appearances and Ascension

During a forty-day period after his resurrection, Jesus appeared to his disciples to ensure them of his continued presence and to give them instructions for the future. He would ascend to heaven, he explained, and while he was there, the disciples were to continue to spread his message. Jesus commissioned his followers to make disciples of all nations by baptizing and teaching them everything that he had taught. The ascension is necessary, Jesus continued, because "unless I go back to my Father, the Holy Spirit will not come to you" (see John 16:7).

Pentecost and God's Presence

The Spirit came ten days after Jesus's ascension. It happened on the day that we now call Pentecost. The Spirit came with a power that enabled the ministry of Jesus to continue through his disciples. The Spirit brought the presence of God in a way that was unlimited by space and time.

Pentecost and God's Power

After God's Holy Spirit had descended upon each of Jesus's followers, he gave them a boldness to preach the gospel. The gospel is the good news about God's new covenant through his Messiah Jesus with all people. The first time the disciples preached, people from everywhere, who were assembled in Jerusalem for the Pentecost festival, heard the gospel and were moved to conversion—three thousand that first day. Before long the gospel spread far beyond Jerusalem, and the church became a powerful reality in the world.

The Holy Spirit and the Growth of the Church

This rapid growth of the church created a strong opposition. One of the primary opponents was a Pharisee named Saul. In spite of his young age, he had gained great prominence among the Jewish leaders. One day, on his way to Damascus to track down and persecute more Christians, a powerful vision of the resurrected Jesus stopped him. This encounter radically convinced Saul of the truth of the Christian message, and it led him to conversion and baptism. He then changed his name to Paul. After a season, a prominent church member named Barnabas, who was ministering in the church in Antioch, called on Paul to come and help him there.

Church Growth and Church Conflicts

This ministry in Antioch gave impetus to the conviction that God wanted the gospel to be preached to all people everywhere. Paul and Barnabas now left the church in Antioch to take a journey into Asia Minor to spread the good news. Upon their return, Paul and Barnabas found that some Pharisees were vehemently opposed to their ministry, although they had acknowledged that Jesus had come from God. These so-called Judaizers preached that people could only become Christians if they would also keep the law of Moses. Paul and Barnabas were infuriated! To them the new covenant was a covenant of Spirit and faith, not of law and rituals. The so-called gospel of the Judaizers was no gospel at all.

Finding the Focus for the Christian Faith

To settle the matter, Paul and Barnabas went to talk to the leaders of the mother church in Jerusalem. In this meeting—after prayer, testimony, and conversation—it was determined that God did not require Gentiles (non-Jews) to become Jews before they could become Christians. By giving his Spirit to the Gentiles, God had already spoken on the matter, they concluded. Everyone who would trust in Jesus's death as atonement for human sin and who would recognize his resurrection as the manifestation of God's power over evil, belonged to God. The evidence that someone had become a Christian was the presence of God's Spirit, not the keeping of the Mosaic law. In this way, the meeting in Jerusalem became the starting point for a powerful mission enterprise that would spread the gospel throughout the world.

Paul and the Global Expansion of the Church

Paul made at least three missionary journeys, starting churches everywhere from the province of Galatia through Asia Minor to Europe. Paul worked tirelessly day and night, preaching, teaching, and writing letters to help the churches stay on track and remain strong in the face of opposition. Hostility was vehement from both within and without. Within the church, false teachers fired their malignant darts in an attempt to pull the infant church away from the gospel message Paul had preached. From outside the church, social and political pressures and the surrounding pagan cultures attempted to crush the new and struggling fellowships. Although the gospel message withstood this animosity, opposition finally caught up with Paul, who was jailed. He used his right as a Roman citizen to have his case tried before Caesar.

Paul's Death and the Unstoppable Gospel

Paul stayed under house arrest for two years in Rome, where he was able to continue a teaching and writing ministry. After this imprisonment, he was probably released for a little while before being taken captive again and martyred during a heavy persecution launched against all Christians by the Roman emperor Nero. This persecution did not stop the spread of the gospel, however. Even when the persecution increased about twenty years later under the Roman emperor Domitian, who demanded that all people call him lord (a title Christians reserved for Jesus alone), Rome could not stop the gospel. Willing to pay with their lives for the good news about Jesus Christ, Christians continued to preach about the grace of God and the presence of his kingdom.

God Brings His Story to His Purposed End

The last book of the Bible speaks to the suffering that God's people often face. At a time when Christians served as prey for wild animals for the amusement of thousands of people at the Coliseum in Rome, the book of Revelation gave

Christians a glimpse of what was to come. Suffering will not last forever! God will honor his promise and vindicate his people. He will create a new heaven and a new earth, where all evil will have no access. Those who have received his Spirit, and become a part of his people in this life, will come to enjoy his full presence forever.

The presence of God and the coming of his kingdom, which is now experienced in part, will then be experienced in full. Those who through faith in Jesus enjoy God's fellowship in this life will end up where humanity began, alive in the full presence of God, where they will see him face-to-face. The story will end where it began—God and humans together in close fellowship. God will completely restore the fellowship that humans destroyed (Genesis 3).

The Power and Purpose of This Story

Why tell this story? We tell this story because it is more than a story, even more than just a true story. It is *the* story! It is a story that better than any other story makes sense of life. It gives coherence and structure to our understanding of the universe. It gives meaning to our experiences and direction to our decisions. It gives human beings a clear identity. It is a story that has the power to reestablish the true quality of the humanness of life. It refuses apathy! It requests a hearing! It petitions to be internalized! It's a story that promises a life-changing encounter with God!

Stories and Human Self-Understanding

Our lives as human beings are made up of stories that have shaped, or are shaping, who we are. The story of the Bible has the power to make sense of all the other stories of your life. When it is internalized, and it becomes a sounding board for your story, it gives meaning in the midst of meaninglessness and value in the midst of worthlessness. Your personal story will find grounding in creation, guidance in crises, re-formation through redemption, and direction in its destination. People truly become Christians when their own stories merge with, and are understood in the light of, God's story.

© **Preben Vang, 2019**